Milk for Gall

Milk for Gall

Natalie Louise Tombasco

Winner of the 2023 Michael Waters Poetry Prize

Published by the University of Southern Indiana
Evansville, Indiana

ISBN: 978-1-930508-58-3   First Edition

Printed in the USA

Library of Congress Control Number: 2024945752

This publication is made possible by the support of the Indiana Arts Commission, the National Endowment for the Arts, the University of Southern Indiana College of Liberal Arts, the USI English Department, the USI Foundation, and the USI Society for Arts & Humanities.

Southern Indiana Review Press
Orr Center #2009
University of Southern Indiana
8600 University Boulevard
Evansville, Indiana 47712

sir.press@usi.edu
usi.edu/sir
Ron Mitchell, Rosalie Moffett & Marcus Wicker, eds.

Artwork: Winnie Truong; *winnietruong.com*
Layout: Zach Weigand & Pandora Wells

Contents

BULB REALM

"But doth suffer a sea-change
Into something rich and strange."

William Shakespeare, *The Tempest*

"And this is the kingdom you bore me to,
Mother, mother. But no frown of mine
Will betray the company I keep."

Sylvia Plath, "The Disquieting Muses"

Drawbridge + Moat

I do these / Things which I do, which please /
No one but myself. **Marianne Moore**

Gingerly, yes,
With the intactness
    Of a walled city or coaxed throat that's been hinged open
    By ginseng. I begin with a primordial sigh

Like when Sappho
Lets go of fragments; wind-
    Fetch rushing land as wet vengeance. Sighs are swimming in
    River mud with frog spawn. Sighs are walking in petti-

Coats and ancient
Shoes. The golden bough
    Lets go all resignation in bride-white sighs. The lyre
    Accumulates a sighful impediment. Wingéd

Chariot—too
Fussy? I speak in this
    Secret language, passive as if *things just happen*, but
    I swear, by the end, I'll be draped in sighs like ermine

Upon a heap
Of rime-royal, Oxford
    Commas. Aristocratic pugs eat from this soft plain:
    My hand. Good boy, *good*. My sex is a semicolon—

I will never
Properly know how to
    Use it. Who doth make the rules? Queenhood will breed grave dis-
    Appointment. I have hips; sue me. All my sighs will be

Celibate, joust-
Ing lances charge any
    Foreign breach. Such a sheepish renaissance with all its
    Overtones, undertones, Ulyssessing. Ugh, poet-

Ess! What is my
True utterance? Is it
    A grunt? a nag? I am quite afraid the moat will break,
    The rush that sets spiel into motion. It's all over

For you hoes when
I mix Glory into
    My night cream—devastate thine enemies. There will be
    No Romantic verticality, no Icarus

Cloudward leap. God,
These v. expensive
    Lipstick tubes melt. Only earthly things, where a sigh may
    Open up in the ground any second. Now I ride

Through a semi-
Permeable membrane:
    Plush red bed. Is it time for a quest? I've spent all week
    In uncomfortable shoes; I'd like a little rest.

concrete realm

Peonies in Utero

I follow a strange bloom with slender limbs:
the signature pink & plush reek of a peony. Stalk

her into sweet smells of confession, spring,
morning moon, a white budding tree near the lake.

I begin by washing my feet, drinking an indigo elixir.
At first timid, she tells me about hard, cracked dirt,

the ho-hum life among swans & the reasons we
prune the dead. Somehow her femaleness offends me

in a Kate Moss, small-breasted, dark-rooted sort of way.
I think she feels my discomfort or guilt. She tells me

vile truths: I cannot keep a fiddle-leaf alive.
I threw my baby dolls in the dumpster.

I am used-up, scraped-out. I feel myself growing
colder, cumbersome, thunderstruck with grunge

about to crack into a whole garden of bolts:
Bring me the closed heads of peonies on a platter.

She folds like a parasol & collapses to a sprout
back into wet dirt. I do not know who or what

I am made from—if my body can ever be home
to a wheatfield. I begin pinning thoughts upon

the clothesline: being one woman is never good
enough. We were the same, clipped from the same

deep pink root. I could feel her, rogue peony,
settling down, flowering from my mouth.

Lolita's Dissection

In the deli parking lot, we were those bestial babes—
gutting a White Owl, blowing its insides out
onto an undercover cop car.

Without the moon's help, we were girls becoming
holographic jailbait. *Hey, mister, be a dear & buy us
some beer.* Our mothers still postpartum.

Don't be short with me! we screamed at the night.
Girls like euphemisms waiting to happen. A vague
rain. We were transactional sex. *Cha-ching!*

We were kiss-him-because-he's-so-goddamn-boring,
a mouth breather. Remember how we watched lava
lamps through needle holes, became feline,

nectarine fizz in our jewel-like heads? Remember
being stripped lollipop pink & spread on a strange
bed? Love was always like this, jagged & hooked

to a different mouth. In morning's eggshell,
we were those girls who slept late
with valedictorians. Promising girls, going

places. Intended to keep our animals secret,
but we were those amphibious nymphs: green
& splayed   pinned down on a nerd's dissection tray.

Collective Invention

René Magritte, 1934

girl, what's the fishmonger to do with you?

on the shore of Nantucket   forget scrimshaw,
forget Venus on her scallop stage—   you're a product
of a madman: half mackerel, half pubic hair—

hooked & hauled   dredged up from God
knows where   hush now   think of the mermen you've teased
pray for some oilskin   to take you away as commodity

my prophecy?   they'll make sashimi of you
a rich man's nyotaimori   along your canvas-flat thighs

goody goody gum drop   my tentacles are flaring up!
but I'm tired of my animal   aren't you?

quit acting so washed-up & helpless
embrace your inner fish freak

stand upright   flounder into a coffee shop
let your widemouth say   *a vanilla latte & quiche, please?*

whatta riot!   I wonder which is more disturbing:
your fins or femininity?   go give blush to the prudes
go slip on a pair of tube socks—   you're more than pretty paradox

go wonder if the sea still moves
                              without you there

Deadbeat Beach

what have you given me
besides the rotten bottom of the pot,

this salty, deathbed pawnshop
of carapace, fish guts, red Solo cups,

syringes and tampon shells?
I'm feeling like the Audubon

of feral cats and a thousand paper gulls
as the sea swells swallowing the marsh;

I am collecting Wonder
Bread bags thinking about carnal love

with the eye of a diving-suited curator,
rambling, "I am she: I am he"

while standing in the muck
of a horseshoe crab orgy; your love

is hypodermic, full of wreckage,
and I'm rummaging for loveliness

like a mother lode of salt-spray roses
or beach plums or an egret

who walks like a minute hand.

Ferry Song, Half-Sung

Whatever your vernacular—
I'm gacked on it: clouds cracking up, crump
of brown paper bags on beer cans.
Listen, let me get a baconegg&cheese, AriZona
iced tea & a Newport behind the ear.
Gimme your liquor, your lotto tickets,
your shredded lettuce. Jackpot, burner phone.
Gimme your lowbrow meow, blue-collar

slang, all the Wu-Tang-loving white boys
on The Island, where the question is dead ass
& the answer is dead ass. Your sound is fiberglass,
nylon. Acrylic nails tapping against the windows.
If you see something, say something. All right,
I'll say it: boat ride of morning or night, boat ride
of keeping the 99% out & we're all praying
that God might pluck us from this hellhole

with the little anchovy fork of an Ortiz jar.
Staten Island Ferry, you found your place,
the in-between—Dante's wet dream—
as Creamsicle bada-bing, as neon-lit stream,
or as goldfish in the bowl; your orange
has all the passengers rooting for you
like Seabiscuit of the harbor & somehow
I'm always running through announcements,

Downtown 1 Train to South Ferry,
through the beatbox of yellow cabs,
through stairwells of warped saxophone,
hopping the turnstile in a tread of Timberlands,
stomping the life out from alliums
in Battery Park. I'm staring up
the bronze snout of *Charging Bull,*
running through Daniel Pantaleo motherfuckers

        & Dad's voice saying *Don't give authority any lip*,
dipping by the guys selling tourists a ticket
     to Ellis Island, but they can tell
by my don't-talk-to-me face & ugly
     service-worker shoes that I'm not for sale.
I'm like Melanie Griffith in *Working Girl*,
     except less cawfee, less schlep, less red-
lipstick schmear. Ferry, listen, the longest

     relationship I've had is with my MetroCard,
holding it dear in my pocket. Place a cupped ear
     to the ground, hear the skulls that gave in
to sidewalk. Listen to the waves going *hallelujah*,
     hollaback. Do you get my spindrift?
Honey nights: song of hustle, of bailout, of being
     mad tight—it carries us over, kills me with dank
kush delight. Your song won't be lost.

The Promenade, Brooklyn Heights

oh god it's wonderful / to get out of bed /
and drink too much coffee / and smoke
too many cigarettes / and love you
so much **Frank O'Hara**

I lurve/loave/luff you
I've turned cinema junkie for your dicey placeness
decade-long courtships in the vein   of Harry & Sally
& "I'll have what she's having"   & "We are here to ruin ourselves"
          & Brooklyn   "I want you to get   in my bed"

    I'm trauma-bound to you
    your water towers   your pigeon king who coos on a roof
    how it is always the season of yellow
          as in turmeric-stained wooden spoons   no yellow
          as in Jamaican beef patty

in postcoital introspection   I want you to call me Daphne
of the Delicatessen: latkes   lox & leeks   the quintessential
pastrami on rye   splitting out of myself like a seed   planted
on the corner of Pierrepont Place   & Montague Street

I'm twisting into bark   gnarled & neurotic as night   O Brooklyn
your hunt is heavy in my branches
                     & I'm hella stuck
in your dirt   in my confliction of rooting   or fleeing

Dyker Heights, 2017

Winter sneaks up,
slips through your skin.
Out the window
an abrupt crunch
of its black boot on white.
It's a grumpy neighbor
chewing on life.
In the yard, you leave warm
milk for the stray thing
pussyfooting around.
In the bowl, it abandons
one small hair
as if to say *thanks.*
The hush-hum heat rattles on.
You want to go out, stay in.
Knock-knock. All the parties are going:
string lights and schnapps,
the kindle of talktalktalk
and fussbustle and tinselkiss
and giftglow and
someone making snow
angels on the hardwood floor as you ghost
out because icicles
are more your speed.
You're stuck in a clear spike,
a slow drip
off the roof. Time blooms
daggers from a fountain.
You drift off the porch, onto the road
where the first snow
suffocates potholes. On worn tires,
winter lurks so quiet
you never look over your shoulder.

Dream Vision Descending Into Dickinson

"I opened the Door" "to your alabaster planet" "*hit a World, at every plunge*" "slumped down & down" "a sleep-warm tunnel" "that was Amherst-winter-dark" "felt like Victorian lace curtains" "the voices" "dispersed" "as I fine-tuned my dreaming" "to labor" "in four-beat, three-beat" "down-feathered hymns" "safe in this underground chamber" "of train tracks, tenor & vehicle" "souls with pocket watches" "perpetually late" "velvet heads streaming Grand Central" "I grew accustomed to the light" "pouring through Windows" "poor janitor, mopping up" "maelstroms of white dresses" "but I am a visitor" "my business is theft" "I stole the 'eat me' Crumbs" "none are left" "the Closet said, 'we've been expecting you'" "& so I crawled through" "your Society:" "the garden district" "of fetal petals" "veiny wonderland" "forgetting myself minute by minute" "Hope dug its ostrich head in the sand" "'can you re-mother me?' I asked" "the somebodies" "but they were mercury-brained" "gap-toothed gladiolus" "rude animals" "a powder-wigged Newfoundland" "asked 'who are YOU?'" "*I'm nobody! who are you?*" "*are you*" "*nobody*" "*too?*" "blew hookah circumference in my face" "the best way to describe" "a thing" "is to uncover what it is not:" "a house" "is a feminist epic" "a thrush" "is a tyrant" "the divine creator" "is a bird-boned girl" "then the tailor" "handed me a little pilgrim hat" "& escape capsule into the upper world:" "the *I*" "became black ice" "a waxed floor, continuously" "& I *finished knowing*" "*then*"

Hieronymus Bosch's *The Garden of Earthly Delights*

Somewhere between Eden & Hell, Virgin & Venus, I am
the pearl-plink girl being carried away in a mussel shell,
away from sweet-smelling cherry pits, serpents mingling

with tendrils, away from the soft porn that goes on inside
giant strawberries—pricks of leg hair, pulsating seeds—
away from carouseling anti-vaxxers, doomsday preppers

& constitutionalists, the genetically modified Antichrist
germinating within a broken eggshell. A greedy little man
gouging the flicker & spark & *eureka!* of underground

magical black stuff. O triptych of thick-tongued chaotic,
where do you hinge? Father taught me to tend the tilth,
to deadhead paradise on anything unzipped, unfurling,

on fleshy figures frolicking, mewing cutely in their amniotic
bubble world. I've dipped a toe into that wasteland spacescape,
so groovy & pyro-dream: charred black from consuming

boreal forests, Sumatra, LA traffic, the blueprints of trust
fund babes. "April is the cruellest month" I chant; I hyperventilate
into the carpet as the outside gets greener, meaner, even the birds

are distancing as I throw white bread to the ground like
Hello, Clarice. This garden, its blues, greens, browns, goes on
delighting—the sparrow keeps giving her all, stirring song

with paint, but paradise has gone tasteless as a stick of Juicy Fruit.
Whatever happened to the dodo, the great auk, Flint?

Shitshow Barbie

Mattel, bless her with resting bitch face, nippleless breasts, lady parts bare
as those of the little girls who play with her. Bless her with an accessory kit
of Xanax smoothies, anal bleach, a Limited Edition Jade Egg™ & booklet called

How-To Clear Bad Juju from Your Yoni. Bless her with pointed feet
on yellow subway nubs. Shitshow Barbie does Kegels on the 1 Train!
Give her nights full of gasoline & glitter, parties at the Collapsible Rooftop.

Grant her the ability to keg stand longer than Hipster Ken, to vomit—
wash it down with gin & tonic. A little voice that when closing her bar tab
says *Math is hard!* Nights that pull at her fishnets. Bless her with deep

purple mouth-mashing on fire escapes, the strength of paralysis
when Ken's plastic fingers touch her too hard 'til she's swollen & bleeds
all over the bathtub. Girls, remember the red is love! Mattel, name her

the Patron Saint of Getting into Bad Situations with Questionable Boys.
Bless her with disheveled mysticism. Shitshow Barbie can get on bruised knees,
pray away a brushfire of sin. Girls, press her battery-operated voice box

& all night she'll question: *O Cool Pope, is there still time for my sainthood?*
O Father of Sticking Pins, why did you manufacture me this way?

Girl in Bathtub, Flicking Dried Rose Petal

Notice the unlocked door. Edward Hopper voyeur,
     peer through the keyhole:
       regal, a vision—O buoyant breastbone, the hillside of knees
         in honeysuckle & milkweed! O foreplay, forefinger
         tracing through foam & steam.

   So much of a girl's time
                  is spent

pruning, waiting for someone to come eat her. So much of a girl's time is spent being
   a catalyst
     for sin in silk & fringe.

Watch as she marks territory with bobby pins: backseat, nightstand, sink basin.
Watch as she swells under the hot spell.
        Boudoir, from the French, meaning a woman's room
       for sulking in   to pout   prettydaysaway.

Notice how all she wants is to get clean   together, how all she wants is someone
to be hyphenated to.
              Ignore that time is measured by a lighter's fluid.

Notice how she's both demure   & stink eye.
Listen as she sighs   at mildew & grime, waiting for
       her body to materialize.

Q Train

Nigel Van Wieck, 1990

Half-note, hairpin—pungent, dried-up sexpot
on the orange & yellow seats, slumped in thought.

The tunnel critters are her only friends & foes.
Lonely, lovelorn moonbeam—washed-out redhead.

Sundown, daybreak—sleepwalk, pass out. Wake up (!)
to a strangeman's hand, the taxi-cab rhapsody—

5 a.m. halal truck, bodega. This is the subway sutra:
late night transfer, Merlot smolder. *Tsk-tsk,*

suckteeth, eyeroll, spreadlegged—feral realist:
the muse on the Staten Island Ferry drinking

a forty. A white girl's manifesto begins: *I can't even.*
Dog days, young love—gut punched, worn-out mystic.

Putrid midnight, skylines, bloodlines—inside,
she holds a sinkhole, an orchid. The feminist-

approved odalisque—she gives the world the cold
shoulder. This place is trying to ruin her.

Dream Vision of Theodore Roethke

door to heaven? portal of wheres in a modern mound. to be skinned alive and dolled in moss (spongy and yellowish like sheet cake) would be ideal; desecration in reverse. the soil is shut-eye dark, no matter. once the dirge of scattered wetness ends, the roots go from sinew to delicate,— untangle and plummet with gravitational urge to the Snail Domain; they carry truth on their backs. is this where the old florist lives in his tendrilous shoes? why are graves so darn slippery? who is it that said to me: die? I'm looking for mother mildew, father fear. the fat slug cried, you have to take a little responsibility, dear. *pipe-knock, fish nerves.* lulled by the verve of sibilance and fricative, the fungi's ennui,—into root cellar's labyrinth of parsnips,—oh lull me into a biscuit smeared with perverse preserves: my soul was not spotless, but I knew the sadness of rutabaga. a bulb-shaped loneliness that waited for you, fermented in the rank ditch under barometric pressure. *this is my hard time.* crude weather accumulates in the bones. creaking, cracking, finally veering to breathless green,—oh hothouse: cannas, orchids steaming up the glass on a winter night. I'm a fiddleheaded epiphyte. *this way! this way! imitation, conscious imitation* in the Kingdom of Soft-Sighs. are you my lost pearl? will you teach me how to study the lives on a leaf? tether me to your glass womb under the germinal moon; I will wait

Still Life with Navel Orange

Glam-glowing navel w/ intrusive malformation:
linea nigra, a vertical line rising on its swollen peel.

i. the study

Darling orange, I shall call you Belladonna
for the pretty poison thoughts you've allotted.
I touch the flank of me—animalistic, delicate—

in morning's twisted bedsheets where I am nectar
& big bang creation, imploding with ideas like
a roadside bounty. I could be more than this half-

person if I wanted, if I didn't backtrack for miles
to girlhood: when things were perfectly dumb, before
I could think of bad things like barefoot & pregnant.

I was Mother's little helper, little thumbsucker,
everything tasted like nail polish & cigarette butts.
I had an oral fixation—felt my tongue as it learned

that *clinical* rhymes with *cynical.* Before I knew
what my body could do, what men could do: unteach
the bunny ears on your shoe. What germinated

in the black of the laundry room? If vulnerability
is what you crave, I know pressure points. I know a man
never wants a woman after he's watched her give birth,

after the dark twin of herself comes out shitting
& screaming. O orange, you are so purposeful—
an alchemist of any mistake. How do you choose

between lunchbox love notes & morning papers?
I whisper monsters & moonlit forests into your belly,
but never physics or theorems or spheres.

I say: *Dearest Seedling, you'd never be the glue that holds*
Daddy & me together. For I am an uninhabitable ravine—
the dank smut of supernova debris & fruitful fuck ups.

ii. the fleshing out

Uncertain if I'd destroy you in entirety—let you
dwell in belly—if I'd collect your teeth & fingernails.
If I'd mark your height on the wall,

say stuff like *You're so cute I could eat you.* Orange,
in your splendor, sweet umbilicus of sin—I want
to dissect you, breach your skin, carry your zest

beneath my nails. I feel your weight in my palm—
your lovesome marmalade of curls, then the eventual
bitter: *I fucking hate you* as you slam the front door.

Stupid orange, I cannot undress & swallow you
like a drug—for you are someone else's masterpiece:
unlike Rubens' baroque *Saturn* beautifully sucking

the life force from his son, more so Goya's torchlit
devouring, each limb burrows into mouth's soft cave.
Crazed and with brute force, I break you right

at the soft spot in your skull where lives the plot,
the prophecy to usurp, only to unearth the lame
taste, your membrane between my teeth.

Bees!

Honey-drudgers. / I am no drudge **Sylvia Plath**

Bees yellow as Twinkies swan dive into wisteria.
Colony collapse is her primal scream: orange
Blossom, alfalfa—gone spindly in pesticides,
Monoculture disease. Where is the royal jelly,
The lavender fizz, that good good Tupelo honey

From a backwoods swamp & sold on I-65
With a biscuit? Where is the bee hum?
Little socialist kazoos. Blame the husbandry,
The un-wilding, conquering. It is not pleasing
To Caesar that the wind does not curtsy,

That I control meltwater. Blame Monsanto's
Patented seeds. Supermarket piles of plump
Pummelos, green lawns cut into square feet.
Listen to spring's oracle: daffodil's lulling
Of slugs. A contagious hush. It is a ruthless

Silence, brutal, but lovely as birth control.
Outside it is a blue April. Inside there is *Silent
Spring* & *Slow Violence*. Will the hive survive
On Tate & Lyle? Is childbearing best when
Scientists forecast a decade left? I squeeze the life out

Of a plastic bear. I'm in a swarmy mood. Not even
The beekeeper's smoke can shut me up. Is a woman
Just an egg-laying machine confined to her den,
Surrounded by radiant jars of viscous manuka
As the Hollywood sign is carried away in mudflow?

Brown sugar, molasses, hibiscus. The swarm is going
Berserk in their smallness, their superorganism.
Industrious virgins of rosehip hocus-pocus, warning
To wake the fuck up & smell the mint leaves, clementines,
The withering—*hurry!* before the soil settles into elegy.

Lust-Drunk

A fool for thinking I could eat mango
over the sink without feeling a thing.
Costanza said of the sunlit stimulant
"I feel like I got a B12 shot!" but picture it: in summer's
late light, belligerent, the dark kitchen, I probed the ripe
skin with a dirty butter knife. I felt for tenderness,
never asked consent for its nakedness. Felt for
a brief moment as if I were Jeffrey Dahmer, in the serial
I-want-to-keep-this-inside-me-forever
kind of way. This isn't supposed to excite, or get panties
in a bunch, like a first-date gut punch, when you both
realize: *I'm a nerd for you* and *This is someone
I can watch* Seinfeld *with* and you're both hungry
for flesh, so you mash those cottonmouths together
in the awkward quiet of a parent's basement.
You both accept that this person is likely to take off,
perhaps due to a mid-life crisis, or the afterlife,
while you are left listening to the sweet nothings
of the garbage disposal.   I've wondered why violence =
masculine and nymphomania = feminine, and done
the math on how many orgasms are being faked
this very second, all while at the grocery store,
carrying a single basket containing a single mango,
because that's just the type of person I am.
Pitiful, really, to go at a mango, ravenously
hickeying its sweet meat down to the stringy bits
as juice runs along my elbow and into the dishwater
like an inkblot test, resembling the silhouette
of Costanza's stout body on a velvet couch, and my skin
gets sunwarm for his black dress socks and bald spot.
I'm liquored up, pent up, gluttonous—when some brilliant
killjoy comes along: God's way of saying *That's enough*
as the slippery pit lies limp in the sink. I fingerlick and beg
for an easy fix, waiting for a yellow jolt, something
to go aflutter like a small kiss behind the ear.

The Curious Sadness of Sugar Cone

enough gibbous vanilla & rainbow sprinkle—space junk, sugar funk. enough in the trunk,
the plump, jiggle & chafe. goodbye, love handles. goodbye, honey high. imagine how difficult
it must be to soulcycle when you're cone-shaped. hello, recipe card box—may i feed you
something pretty? hello, laxative, can i stomach you? i've engulfed a heap of self-loathing,
a cherry on top. hey there, ketosis & halitosis. oh, osteoporosis—hollow me
out. my sickness beats your sickness. hello, infertility—i want this line
to wither, to rot. welcome bareboned, concave conquest. bring on
skeleton-me. bring on mood-moon phases. enough sadness that
spills from me—dropped, forgotten cone on a sidewalk. i will
sulk on a scale, blow up a bmi chart. this isn't about
nicole-richie-skinny, or heroine-chic. farewell
fructose binge, farewell fullness! form,
i will purge you of hurt. goodnight
fifty-calorie being. goodnight little
voice that goes: *fatfatfat.*
sleep tight, bosomhood.
enough being atlas.
i want to be cosmic
dust. i'm just
tired of hold-
ing onto so
much.

Elegy for Anthony Bourdain

Gastronomy is the science of pain.

I want to slurp a never-ending bowl of spicy noodles
    & ride in a train car on the edge of the Himalayas
as the greens of a deep valley saturate my laptop screen

to follow you into the dark tunnel of forgotten places
Beirut   Madagascar   Detroit

& from my parents' house I watch late
    into the morning
        your underwater escape
from a straitjacket to a kitchen table

the table has a topography
temporal // imaginal // borderless

where your philosophy is plated
with phyllo dough & a glug of good
olive oil

    food is storytelling   communion—
You gotta put something in your mouth to get your ears open

I imagine you as a father
perpetually gone on a business trip   maybe in Provincetown

this time—   the last stop on the hook
about to wash away into the Atlantic   someplace

a deep-fried dreamscape
beautifully desolate & hypnotizing
as a machine stretching saltwater taffy & you—
dishwasher or oyster shucker—   homesick   seasick
& growing back sea legs

as each episode ends it is as if vacation is over
I'm a child being unbuckled from the car
& carried off to bed

Brief List of Things That Will Kill Me

i. being favored

Contessa, ever-loving oyster shucker: my geography is lying
facedown on ice like a national treasure. Plucked from the Long

Island Sound, I'm the Jackie O of the mollusk kingdom.

I drip Americanness and wait patiently for us to lip-lock,
but lately, you have appeared a bit stabby, as if I am not

symmetrical—a collision of porcelain and gold leaf.

I have slouched around in this ridiculous corset soaking in
your brutal silence for weeks now. Absurdity, how she rode

in on horseradish from some foreign land and tore up the lawn,

how she lives in the guestroom, rent free. I have lost the plot.
Still, I court you with champagne and Queen Anne's lace,

but somehow you distort me, view me through a fisheye lens

where I'm no longer in Lanthimos' sea-light. Once I thought
this usurpation is *so us*, until you began calling me by the new

confidante's name to rub the gout from your feet. I have fallen far.

O codswallop—I'm a pearl-clutch away from tantrums
and questionable survival tactics. To be honest, I hate her

shine and shtick, how I've been supplanted as disposable.

I hate how you bend and warp, how you've turned lapdog.
Darling girl, what makes you tick? If you suddenly become sick,

seek me with your thick tongue and dagger. Hinge me open
like an envelope. *Sigh*—how my complications multiply.

Consider the Lobster Telephone

now look, it speaks as an object of gustatory
pleasure & pain—menacing antennae as if
some trickster, some mustachioed man

—think of it, *aphrodisiac telephone*:
growing off the black rotary like a tumor

or lusting you into bed—see how the mouthpiece
aligns with genitalia & it holds claws close
to whisper the ocean into your ear—genteel little

conversationalist, keeping you on ice
in the bathtub with champagne—with phony

reluctance, it leads through a phosphorescent terrain
to the bottom-of-the-ocean dwellers, scavengers
living on anything semiconscious, semiprecious

—like the one time you ever won anything
it was from a dark tank & named Ruby

you ran across six lanes of traffic to the harbor, setting
the rubber-cinched creature free—but what is there
to do with half-remembered love

do memories feel pain or decompose
or molt or hibernate off the New England coast

at twenty-five fathoms—diving suit,
winter-sleep deep—some argue when you eat
a crustacean's flesh you taste the repressed:

its desire, the unbearable green anguish—
you carry one home in a brown bag

        & in an act of intimacy, reconsider plunging
        the knife between its frantic eyestalks
        as lobotomy, as courtesy—in reconsideration

the do-it-yourself boiling-alive method
appears most humane as you clarify

        butter, do your best to ignore
        the thrasher, lid-clanker—alarming armor
        going tongue-red in hair-raising

needle-screeching suspense
if this becomes too much, walk away

        set a plastic timer for twelve minutes
        goosebump & shook—look over
        your shoulder when the landline *riiiiiiiiiiiings*

once, then twice
& beseechingly answer *hello*

        now look: I was carapace & there was nothing
        but filth specks—I ate the parts others wouldn't eat,
        I ate things I would rather not share

spindle realm

Gnaw at the Orchids

Remember being fourteen, the Queen of Mean?
Stun-gunning with speech? I know about misled anger: boil

cauliflower within an inch of its life. Tell a friend to drop dead,
buzzcut the carpet, bust down the door of a dream. Waking up

is foul milk. *Yuck!* Curbstomp a lotus, implode with childhood's
muck. Childproof your insides. Gnaw them raw—they're tougher

than they look. Orchid your kid. Feed her an ice cube.
Pinkspawn thrives off oakbark's neglect. Ball gag the moon;

snarl it to smithereens. Cry like a hammer—nails puddle the room,
pelt down a staircase and flood the house. Fizzle out, grow smaller,

sorrier, rabbit-hued. Multiplicitous in perennial regrets. Those days
of stayawaystayaway—*Stay, won't you play with my hair?*

There, there. Gather from dirt a bolus of hurt, swallow it.
Seethe green—no dessert unless you drink your kerosene.

Nomenclature

Today's new words are the following: *Grass* is a mounted
video camera usually in dark alleys or near ATMs in order

to catch someone of wrongdoing :: Thankfully, because the mayor

has increased spending on *grass*, authorities were able to find
the suspect who failed to pay his subway fare. *Mountain* is a small

object of blown glass placed upon papers to keep

from a disturbance :: *Mountains* are often collected for hobby.
Foghorn is a long commercial shown between 1:00 to 6:00 a.m.

to sell blenders and memory improvement courses :: She became

reliant upon turning on *foghorns* to find sleep. *English muffins*
have a nightmarish taste, like falling in an elevator. It doesn't matter

how much well-tempered butter is spread into the nooks

and crannies. *Stingray* is a white tablet to temporarily
eliminate sensation :: The headache was so bad, I spilled

a whole bottle of *stingrays* on the bus. *Extinction* is what

Girl Scouts sell door to door for financial literacy
and badges. *Rivers* should be hand-rolled and smoked slow

after a long day :: *Rivers* are contemplative and offer sage advice.

Paradise is an antimicrobial used in the treatment
of open wounds :: Every time I scrape my knees, Momma

pours *paradise* on the cut and it burns real bad.

Down, Down from Fenneltown

In heaven or universe or cosmos jelly, I swam purposeless.
When becoming earth-me, I found myself at Mom's table

doing homework, studying, oh I don't know—
convergent evolution—as she cleaned dirt from the white,

bulbous body of a fennel. She taught me nourishment.
But in secret, between her and the soup, she shared a glass

and a glass and a glass. During the meal we split,
I watched her eyes glaze—go white water, go drunk.

She had gone off again. But to where? Was it a cypress-
winding dream where people said *finocchio* and the wind

tasted like licorice? I hoped her place was that pretty,
was worth it. Isn't it funny how we choose

the body which will carry us, the body which we will carry?
As I stared into her prismatic eye, her squid eye—

realizing how we were from different planets, the same planet—
she asked in her way, *O fennel-chested girl, isn't it strange how*

we've picked one another from a whole galaxy of green fern?

The Girl with the Appetite of an Ogre

Oh ferngreen girly girl, you've chewed Mother up
real good—her cartilage & sinew—gorged on
her freckles, your own blood. What a predicament.

What is your alibi? You've engulfed something
beautiful, tortured, remorseless—something like
the Atlantic. Swallow air to hold down her spit & acid-

drenched ear. Your hiccups sound like her saying
I heard that. It's a shame you're being hollowed-out,
femurs & arteries gone. She sits in your gut, sucking

the last of the intestines through a paper straw.
Bigbad girl, you tried to embarrass her
into change, but you needed animal tracks

leading to fuchsia chrysalis, to love.

Panna Cotta Pastoral

Overstayed my welcome,
what a bad dinner guest!
Been here since embryo,
not another espresso
—I beg you, it will keep me
up all day. Tired from decades
of white hills, of drinking thorns
& needing secateurs to love you.
This hasn't been a candyland
good time—gumdrop geraniums,
scrumdiddlyumptious bees.
I've grown a little since then.
Gene Wilder is dead. Been lying low
like a vanilla bean bathing in vodka;
extract my sweet tooth, bury it
beneath a willow. Heartache, toothache
—thanks, nightcap, I'll go drive
into a wall now. I want the real stuff:
urchin & moss & joy. Outgrown
the sweet hold, the girl mold,
I'll drive all night in the afterglow
of letting go.

Dream Vision of Frank O'Hara

it is 4:40 and I'm drenched in moonstone, sequins, fishnets and general getting-out-of-bedness at the corner of 11th Avenue and 30th hoping for something hum-colored. *get in*, you say, *we're looking for goldenrod!* your broken nose points toward the gilded remnants of Saturday. *it's the night like I love it all cruisy and nelly* and we toast to our only pain being champagne, how life is a series of bad haircuts and witticisms, a long drag on a short cigarette. jujubes! *Finnegans Wake!* honey, turn me into viscous paint: de Kooning, demolition, technicolor taboos. that's so dada how the oil leaks, no! my eyeliner resembles a Kline. I'm sort of gutter rat: folding a slice and spilling the hot tubs of pepperoni onto the sidewalk, but trust me, I can do a time-step: be your Ginger. offer bland remarks like Mae. you force feed me bleu cheese olives, blintzes, reels of celluloid to hurry along my refinement. I ask why you never read me your poems and you say it's like inhaling your own flatulence. just like that. *be a little discreet in your desire, disorder, dying.* you fill my coupe with restlessness and myselves split, undulate. one of me buys the Strega. one of me is in a freak accident. one of me is skin-shedding on the High Line. did you ever imagine your bohemian freight trains would be my railroad ecology, yellow foxtail and hawkweed? must Manhattan be fleeting, fabricated, a gold-leafed dream? by now my cheeks hurt—heart eyes, no-moss mind—but we can't stop brooding about our mothers, those useful thorns. suddenly the skyline is brushed across with a silk salmon scarf and you reach for it like the Sistine Chapel but of course the Staten Island Ferry shows and do I have to go when we're having so much fun

Bubbly + Cake

A package sits on the doorstep. Yesterday was my birthday.   Let's celebrate me

getting out of bed.   A package   is sealed, stamped, delivered with my mother's pretty handwriting.

Before ravaging it, calling her, I think of her   bad day,   her home alone, her voice

getting into the liquor cabinet.

                         I leave the package untouched, heavy,

on the table ticking with the thing that kills me.   How much love was squeezed into the box,

how I always feel   hurt/happy/hurt.   How going home for summer break, I'm happy,

but duct-taped with dread.   Here, a concoction   that goes straight to the head.

                         What becomes of unmothered girls?

This is my package to you   little girl, little sister—   you are learning the person who loved you

first   is absent-but-there and will never notice your resentment.   You can't run away yet.

You can't return

to that quiet   dark   liquid   place.   Baby girl, I will hold your feet

to the fire, then kiss them.   Happy birthday—

                                        you are your mother's daughter.

Pomegranate Inn, Portland, Maine

I left the underworld in the rearview: New York skyline upon the land
like a weighted blanket   northbound on I-95 lined with winter-defiant
evergreen   logging truckers carrying bundles of fat-packed   cigars
there's a rumor that laureled angels stroll along Old Port's lampposts
leggy with wick-fire   through narrow walkways carved into fresh snow
                    not wide enough   for an arm-in-arm bon voyage

the Inn's room is like being inside a Matisse
except where's the honey wand? lemon-ginger scones?
                                        I think I could find anchor here
which is what I think in every place I go   a slight draft
comes from the brüt & choppy sea

the nor'easter festers   in J's Oyster's steamers on the half shell
I walk outside to the blue-lit discombobulated birch limbs   effervescent
& ill-prepared with lack of snow tires   I'm Jack London realness
               & there's only one probable direction: grab a chainsaw
become a woman who wears weather on her face
      except it's not in my nature   I'm too olive-skinned too
Call the Super—we need some heat
                         the elements are plotting against me

in a certain light the white of Casco Bay feels blank   soft   nebulous
like hanging on to pieces of half-remembered dreams: dull-pink skies
sea smoke   a lighthouse that ladders into the clouds   or were they
nightmares   transfigured?

                    & in the whale-oil lamplight I learn:
                         every leaving snow   is lovers parting

On Becoming Bertha

I've slept too long in the moonlight, in velvet
    undergrowth, bridled by alien trees, by menacing
    green. Strange climate of where I go soft, limp
for hushed oracles of the frangipani & river toad.

This is merely the honeymoon phase. Follow behind
    my soiled-white-linen trail through the back door
    as the roof closes in. Are you not thirsty for me
to make a house, a home? Here, small offerings: burnt sage,

honeyed decanters & a Stevie Nicks hex; yes,
    I'm in your blood now, your bones—I've been spiking
    your coffee for weeks. I am ripe with foul thoughts:
I come from a long line of women sacrificing, gone batshit,

dark-forest-swallowing women, strong-smelling women
    like cinnamon & rain & dust, tarantella-exorcising,
    volcanic women who aren't forgetting; a long line
of black-toenailed, jagged, cuticle-biting, brandied women

that feel themselves distorting, dissolving. A crusade
    of Berthas, potent with attic, mad, mad for the image
    you thrust upon us as cold, hard mirrors, as green hills,
& buried alive in projections when it is you in candle glow

    & that lunatic-glimmer in your eye.
    Which witch is lame enough to repent?

This is the first death.
I am no longer the girl you first met.

Advice Column

after What Do We Need Men For?:
A Modest Proposal *by E. Jean Carroll*

alexander the great & bust the bloodlust door

of bergdorf goodman & where creepy boys

interlock like the chanel c's & there are datebooks

of dickwads & each waiting to claim & i'm fifth

avenue kinda lost & girl scout promises or knots

or pocket knives because we're all sold out

of tagalongs, fucker & helluva day for hunter

s. thompson & i've had my head between the knees

& kavanaugh-types in pokagon state park & look up

"*mattress performance (carry that weight)*" & "most hideous

men of my life list" & no-good octobers & off with

your pants! *oh!* maître d' escort me back & the pump room

circa 1970 & this little red is razor-sharp & [space]

& tabula rasa & underwater bath sounds & who stops him

from taking all he can to measure his greatness: furs

then silks then moons & x's on the map & even

the yellow poplar leaves zenith beneath us?

Portrait of a Queen with Dirty Martini, Covered in Cat Hair

Once upon a liquid lunch, the Queen of Sourpuss plunged
    into the magic mirror, tunneling down to the Empire
        of Mismatched Glassware. She began to doubt, *who*

was the fairest, after all? Flush as a pimento, she screamed
    at the gilded frame, *I've got purses older than you!*
        & eyerolled her way through woodland creatures,

trampling gnarled groves—what would Marx say of the price
    of apples? She avoided the life-saving kisses, the necrophiliacs.
        What she needed was Andy Cohen, a botox frown,

an expensive skincare routine. She needed answers.
    The Queen of Compact Mirrors arrived at the glass lagoon.
        Out from sharp waves, the Old Wives appear hooded,

glistening—as if they have concluded treaties with whelk.
    The thing about Old Wives are their violet eyes & how
        they enter rooms mouth-first, singing katydid hymns.

One Wife turns into a ferry & shuttles them across a century
    towards the Guarded Place. The queen can only think copper
        thoughts as she bores the Old Wives with her stories,

each one beginning *My stomach growled & then I left.*
    It is in their secret bog place where the Old Wives get comfortable;
        one reveals her housedress & varicose veins, one tweezes

her chin, another slingshots a bra onto the lip of the mantle.
    In this place, they speak in metalanguage like blue-jay gossip.
        Boy, do they pass the Bechdel test. The Queen of Hot Flashes

is served Marlboro Lights, the heart of a sad virgin. Never
    expect a queen to do her dirty work. A throaty storm rolls in
        like the emptying of an ashtray. The leader grunts the signal:

it is time. They walk Her Evilness down a long hallway
    of prismatic wallpaper & doors: rooms of girls, rooms lush
        with flora & fountains, conservatories of deathcomas.

Temptation is wire hangers is napalm is nectar.
    Her Badness digs her maraschino manicure into a reflecting
        coffin, as if to say, *this one.* Up, up to the laboratory,

the Old Wives get to the Bunsen burner: *bee pollen, an eye for an eye,*
    a pinch of jellyfish. The queen needs something of pretty girls,
        starving girls—girls who are withering, weaponlike.

The Replica levitates over a pedestal: succulent larvae
    of dead matter & cold cream. Her Realness thinks of the men
        in her life—mail carriers, henchmen, philosophers—

their heavy breasts, their under-eye bags like pregnancy pillows;
    thinks of how each morning she mouths *olive juice, olive juice,*
        olive juice into the looking glass; thinks of vanity as worthiness,

as something that can't be washed off in an ancient pond,
    as a little reminder, like an old dog, of your replacement; thinks
        beauty is stuck inside a canvas, grown in an incubator,

    or spills, rolls away like marbles on an uneven floor.

Fever Dream Vision of Allen Ginsberg

all aboard! skipper-you releases the cleave hitch and we're off on the black waters of Lethe, leaving behind a wake pattern of deep gossip and starry-mouthed incantations. I'm with you on a pilgrimage to forgetfulness, to be free from toxic habits engaged in with reckless abandon. I'm with you to unknot, unlearn what has caught up. I'm with you eating a kaddish and catfish sandwich, drinking a paper-bagged ferry beer, where we pour foam out for the dead homies. I'm with you haloed in Blakelight as we *toot-toot* through purgatory, under the Williamsburg Bridge where angelheaded girls graffiti cloud-lettered names, who eat wind to cure asymptomatic happiness, who study their mothers chained to a stereotype and get busted feeling sentimental for the enumerations of pummelos, who scroll mindlessly through redpilling rocketmen freebasing hydroxychloroquine, jonesing for Cheetodust rapture. I'm with you but the crew says, *go home America, you're drunk*, but then *it occurs to me that I am America*. I am talking to myself again, so naturally, the ferry slips into a vulgar vortex with isles of cornflake hypnosis and bottles of dead water and I come out jiggling like canned cranberry sauce reincarnated from my signified-berry. I'm with you in full-fledged migraine, shopping for images and wondering the point of writing poetry in white-picket apocalypse? I'm with you howling *I hope this email finds you well* as I'm back in Wichita where Rand cuts the lawn into iambic pentameter and Nance fills me to the gills with potato salad and I run off to the nearest Greyhound station for the first bus out of myself

Lolita's Exorcism

In the backseat of the yellow bus, our heads whirled round
like tops upon gingham frocks. Summer on the cusp
& overnight we bursted into beasts with golden leg hair,

stench, butterfly clips & hip bones that appeared in rooms
before us. In the '90s, we were damn fine, serpentine,
had *lick me* eyes at eleven, split-tongued & stanning for Satan—

peccadilloed our way to someday be a good little host body.
We flat-ironed gyres from our hair, left bloodstains on white couches.
Our mouths stuffed with bars of soap for flinging *twats* & *cunts*

around the locker room like wet toilet paper. *Parasitic perverts*
whispered the world behind our backs, but really we kept
Mr. Rubberwood from jamming sticks into our bicycle wheels.

It seemed, back then, we were a turn of phrase: spiraling out, fatherless,
thinking *nuclear family* meant *mushroom cloud.* Our mothers tried
to restore order, brought in doctors, priests, that studly crucifix. O,

how Mother tossed a box of tampons upon the bed. *Carefully
read the instructions* she said. *That thing upstairs is not my daughter.*
Flew over our handlebars, full stop. A cloud split like an atom.

Who would teach us how to break? Time fell from a sycamore
like helicopter seeds. It blanketed us as we went head-spinning,
headboard-shaking, contorting into teen girls. Didn't we piss on

the front lawn, eat raw red meat during TRL? Rehearsed guttural
shrieks as the wind's wet fingers rubbed circles over wine glasses?
Didn't we carve 666 into wrists & spider-walk down the stairs

in prom dresses, men hiding in the crawl spaces of our chests?
Hadn't Mother warned us? It seems our trial was being enterable,
brassy things with big opinions. Had our blood oath gone

crystalline sacrilege? If evil existed, why did it find shelter
in us as we glittered & danced under the sprinkler's *tsk tsk?*

Juniper + Chest of Apples

Buried the grown-ups beneath the juniper tree. I confess,
tombed bone shards & fed the stew to their silly children.
It was me who sheared away nightfall for a winter coat,
buried my '99 Honda Odyssey behind the shed & caused

a terrible case of root rot, flooding the dirt with pleasantries.
I've devoured dark berries. Never mind my goodness
or wickedness; I'm a girl—watch how I pick up this pen
with my toes. I've preyed on every man with a townhouse

near Gramercy Park, every man who confuses lust
for trust. I bury the men who won't marry, then always
remarry because men can't be alone for a second.
I shovel seedy nursery rhymes & tangle up the stories;

stash away birdsong in the junk drawer while he eats
his joy, his boy—which head
                              should I stitch to my shoulders
today? I lie down in the bed, in mommy's spot. I look *good*.
From this angle, I am True Mother—bloodline & womb.

Reared from a tree hollow where Stepmothers are bred
to obtain maggoty hearts, curdle milk with a look.
A vessel for the butchered psyche of motherhood, plagued
with heavenly depravity. These flaws ferment, rot me out.

I confess, yes, I shut the chest on the boy's head,
but before the millstone gets its revenge, answer this:
What is left for my daughter to inherit? The Catskills,
an acre, thimble? Who blames me?

Viciousness in the Kitchen

you can tell how enslaved the women of any country are by the kind of preparation their traditional foods require. **Louise A. DeSalvo**

To the male poet who told me to replace *women* with something more interesting & to quit writing about food: the kitchen is where all my disorder converges into stewed tomatoes & I eat him by his own light. Girls, Momma ate mortadella all through pregnancy as if to give me a birthmark the size of a pistachio, Grandma taught old-world love & care, my badness through the curse of the wooden spoon & now, I must leave behind the domestic sphere, cauldron & dustpan, witchcraft & blackberry preserves in the cellar—all the feminine cultivation I've had as a measure of staying alive & creating, of traveling & coping. There's viciousness in the kitchen, behind Formica countertops where I tenderize a tenderloin & use a bench scraper to rid me of the thing you said earlier. Whenever I slice into an onion, I think of it as an origin story, as analysand, as "What a thrill— / My thumb instead of an onion." When I mandoline zucchini paper-thin & get my pinky instead & red surges like a riverbed, I think that, finally, I've experienced something. Luckily, I don't need anything to happen when I feel the hint of the blade between the avocado to write it down. Broke as fuck, but I can go go go deep into dashi stock, be tucked away safe in a grape leaf. Dickinson was Vesuvius at Home with metaphysical doors leading into her own geography & so Momma taught me to put on a little music, pour a little wine, to brand my arm on the oven rack as if to say *I'm here* & *I'm moving all at once.* I'm going off to the land I've come from, where San Marzano tomatoes are grown in the fertile soil of Vesuvius' ash & bone—where women are unburied from stationary positions, walk barefoot from the dirt with a little bit of stench, walk as cleaver & fire-bellied things ready to erupt into mouthy manifesto any minute at the *good men*, the male academics who find food frivolous. Didn't your mother teach you not to mess with those that prepare your sustenance? My reflection has festered in the kitchen sick for centuries & I'm tired of peeking out the blinds, of wishing I was small enough to fit inside a Tupperware & I don't care that you've already spoken for the moon.

Take My Milk

Believe that even in my deliberateness
I was not deliberate. **Gwendolyn Brooks**

For gall. For balsam fir.
For tireless bloodhounds

and bear traps of RSVPs. How guilt
bludgeons one like instantaneous

love. Take my continuous O's
for gold rings and garter-belted

teeth and other minor exchanges
here and there. Barter my *va-va-voom*

of biological destiny, the soft and fleshy
Renaissance sprawl.

Rebrand hyper-femme ideal
for vinegar-drinking angels who dominate

indulgences in lieu of holiness,
who study the curvature of a crumb,

a crumb, a crumb, yet play dumb
and "*defeat* 'Nature.'" (*Is this blood*

that stains   my own?
For what throne?) Revise my set-in-stone

choleric disposition. These tired tropes
have gone to seed. Diffuse

my literary dispossession
across this dome like cirrus clouds.

Seize my something borrowed,
something blue

for moon landings. For coronations
in a parallel universe, where I wave

an olisbos-like scepter in the blushed face
of a pathetically out-sonneted errand boy.

Annihilate his lexicon, dislocate it,
abort it within the voice box

and snuff it to a hum. I've decided
to choke the room with baby's breath,

that poor girl's bloom, for advent.
For meteoroids that turn the world

ultramarine as Sassoferrato's virgin,
cerulean by the canful; I bottle the sky

—its vastness, its rifts, and slights—
smear it superstitiously

across eyelids to mimic Neptune's ocean
because "a little water clears us of this deed."

Take my wordlessness for Sybil's leaves.
Caves devour caves, tomorrows empty

into tomorrows. For train tracks. For tunnels
birthing tunnels over centuries.

For umbilicus mundi. For mother tongue.
Mr. Governor, I'll take care of it myself.

bulb realm

To the Sound of Wagner's *Tristan und Isolde*, "Prelude"

after Melancholia, *Lars von Trier, 2011*

(I'm living inside a terrarium: soil, pebble, moss

the world is sick   wind itches like a turtleneck; sea-phlegm

sticks to the shore   I'm trudging through night's tar into the slow burn

of day—where's the upbeat nihilism? I buttered popcorn for the apocalypse

the ultraviolet bees are gone, locusts scuff up my good shoes   *fugue* comes

from the verb for *to flee* or *to chase*   I spent all morning in the shower curlicuing

a strand of hair into an ampersand   I'm saving myself for menopause

I've gone cannibalistic spitting out chunks of my flesh into little fragments

on the lawn   the glass-sky cracks into clouds as credits rain down like

asteroids   I don't flinch at the bright light, or the black & white *Fin*—

I think about my sister   how much I miss her at a time like this)

Swampland with Red Solo Cups

i.

I think of floodlight as moon, as deodand,
as flypaper. Think Ophelia as saint or martyr,

floating in poppies & lilypads & heavy
with drink. Think of landscape as red

wagon, as unspooled cassette tape. Born
from a sigh & malt liquor, we're an island

of youth, frozen, untouched, beautiful—
so edgy with swamp-slick hair, bright-eyed

& bushy-tailed kind of rigor mortis.
Garter snakes slither along darling corpses,

frogs tszuj the messy buns of decapitated heads:
Laura Palmer, Winehouse, JonBenét.

Call us disposable: compost heap in the backseat
of a Jeep, impressionable as a fossil leaf.

Consider us ephemeral glory: lit match,
halo-glow, the blastoff into space.

Live squid tentacles, our names squirm
in your mouth. Our names accumulate,

pulsate with song into a choir of contagion,
bellowing on the bottom of the earth

where Dead Girls know their place:
Central Park, log cabins, milk cartons.

ii.

Little girls are instructed in fear—practicing
cursive like quivering polygraph needles.

Little girls watch Cheerios
tremble in milk like life vests.

Little girls are named after the dead—
name her Natalie: think Natalie Wood

as angular fish, as splendor in the seagrass.
She can't unknow it, her hidden knowledge,

how the water was as welcoming
as a mirror, like an old friend, taking her

away from the yacht to Catalina Island.
Mother says, worst fears are bound to catch up

like blind fish in the midnight zone singing
"That I might drink & leave the world unseen"

—I'm the Dead Girl queen; houseflies linger
on my cheeks, skin rotten, maggots in my hair.

iii.

Hey there little Jeff Goldblum, sing me
your goodnight tune. Panoramic fly,

Goliath-eyed—rubied, black varnish,
blue-green lagoons—swooning,

as the lament begins with
the ceremonial dredging of the lake.

I've written my fascicles, prayed
to the Lord of the Planks.

I'm a witness to this muck-wet affair,
the procession of white snails

with cruel titanium shells.
You can usher the jade moth out,

she did not care for me in life. Leave
condolences on my Facebook wall,

bring pickled fetuses in formaldehyde,
matricide & glitter. Dickinson: mine,

Woolf: mine. My laments are unseen,
lofty as redwoods swelling at damp roots.

Postcard collection, bowl of lionfish,
a single piano key—who will keep

my things? This morning I will drift
beneath a cotton sheet with sickness:

morning, motion, sea & wonder if
I should ghost my mother.

iv.

What if I date boys, a Chatroulette of axe murderers—
Patrick Bateman, Ted Bundy—then quit answering my phone,

maybe they'd decide to kill me for a good reason,
like my long, dark hair? What if my skirt was hiked to the knee,

played the role of Humbert porno fantasy?
What if I had too much to drink, gone red-cheeked—

Brock Turner, Brett Kavanaugh? What if I stopped eating
to disappear in smallness, as penance, as distillation?

What if I locked myself behind Formica countertops,
became an expert wino & never jogged at night—

would I be blameless? What if I consumed hours
of television about detectives in the sex-crime unit?

No matter, I lie cold-blooded in the bone shards
& sludge of the bayou. Just another swamp-slick Betty.

Wiggle your big toe I say. *Now, let's get these other piggies
wiggling.* In a Tarantino foot-fetish scene: follow

my Mary Janes & knee-highs. I am live-oak, teen-girl
magic. Bubblegum & Ouija. The shaved-head version

of Britney, air plants growing
on my wet-warped limbs. I won't apologize

for my stench of honeycomb & catacomb
as I walk from the magnolias with a Doberman

on an emerald leash. I am the Dead Girl drinking
LaCroix next to you in morning traffic.

Dream Vision of Elizabeth Bishop

I journey upon an ancient bus into wet-warped sleep, into *you are an "I," you are an "Elizabeth"*—
from the windshield I register my flora, my geography, my plainspoken diet of poached eggs
and toast and ocean, where under the road's rhythm I drift on and on through soft syllables
spoken by s-shaped birds stuck in mangrove roots, through travelogues that deepen like rivulets
or brainfolds. night's heavy drapes close out the crestfallen cliffs and pinewood dumbstruck
in self-pity, but the dark has runs like afterparty pantyhose. I wear it well. boundaries are
my territory; where it is impossible to differentiate between land and sea, blue from green,
edges from ledges—one body from the next, shadows ajar. all at once comes the celestial jolt:
high beams shine on all 5 feet, 4 inches of her, Lady Precision. with her needlepoint stare I
know I do not belong here. *goddammit*, I rummage through my suitcase like *there's gotta be a
villanelle around somewhere.* she looms. sniffing out something, something, something. a nocturne
that is velveteen. I retreat into the feminine, the Elizabeth wilderness: *why didn't I know enough
of something?* why had the cartographer of my solitude colored my country green, separated
anapests from gasoline? who limited the nature of tides? could *I* be a *house?* white brick, blue
shingles. I must've drunk on an empty stomach again, arguing on the snowy interstate like *baby,
baby get in the car.* my master, with wooly bouffant and steely whisper, dilates, raps the knuckles
with (*Write* it!) and I spill gestures, goodbyes, whole continents on the asphalt like *how do you
hold yourself together?* that's when everything went ice slick, rainbowrainbowrainbow, and she
let me go

Parks!

A landfill could be a time capsule—trove of tchotchkes from the twentieth century: 8-track tape, all seven seasons of *Buffy*, an ex's dingy t-shirt of The Velvet Underground. Wastescape of old wounds: sulphuric & clusterfuck & rank reek that makes you roll up the car window & drive fast over the Bayonne. A salt marsh could be a garbage heap. Origins beginning with the Lenape, Fresh Kills (from the Dutch word *kille*, meaning *riverbed* or *water channel*) was an estuary on northwest Staten Island. It was a breeding ground for oysters, turtles, toads, migratory birds. The Forgotten Borough, as Islanders called it, was the black sheep for its unruly green—no slaughterhouses or factory smoke. Emerson loved it. The island would consume all of the City's trash from 1948 to 2001. The island became *The Dump*; backdrop of a throwaway culture. Container for the metropolis' unwanted residue: bruised plums, the not-so-pretty produce cast off from neon-lit supermarkets. *Shoo shoo*. Out of sight, out of mind. Monstrous, 2200 acres that could be seen from outer space: plastic milk jugs, cheap beer, sporks. Bad memory, erased. *Your dad works at The Dump* said a girl as her father droned about the Dow on the drive to soccer practice. King of the Heap, my father operated cranes atop the gull-gray mountain, came home with oil-stained palms all through the '90s. Slick & hard to hang onto. Pecking away 9 to 5, breathing in methane. When the Twin Towers collapsed, he sifted through *The Pile* for briefcases & body parts while breathing in lead, paint fumes, asbestos. *Shoo shoo* went 1.6 million tons of rubble & steel beams on the last barge headed to Fresh Kills. A landfill could be sacred ground, the kind that makes you do the sign of the cross & a couple of Hail Marys. In the Anthropocene, a landfill can shut its toxic mouth, conceal itself in pliant liners, gas vents, topsoil— become a human-engineered stratum. The Dump could become a park! In a Leslie Knope kind of hope, a return of great blue heron, osprey, muskrats. There will be kayaking & Shakespeare in the Park!

No longer an eyesore or laughing stock. A place for healing, for possibility! But on the park's new soccer fields, I can't get that fresh-cut-grass high I did as a kid. It is summer; the scorched field smells like three-day-old takeout & the black beads of AstroTurf linger in my shoes & hair. Disposable island of hacking coughs & not knowing if Dad will be home. Despite the veneer of sod, I remember that true thing: the hideous stench that is our legacy.

On Being Turquoise

sometimes i'm so extra   so shoulder pads
    & ten-dollar words accumulating in the sky
but my bad, bitch   *baroque* doesn't suit
    today's weather of plain-white-t bluntness:
in less than a week we move   south & so
    i've said the goodbyes, packed feelings into boxes
cloaked myself   in the last roll of bubble wrap
    to be carried out & away & i'm unsure how
i'll manage   without the seasonal moods i've grown
    to rely on. *florida will do you some good.* all that humidity
& vitamin c   although the taste of cantaloupe
    makes absolutely no sense. due to earth's heating
by 2050 london will feel more like barcelona
    & seattle will feel like san francisco
& the real question is   where does that depression go?
    does it migrate north with honking v's of geese?
i've listened to the blue jays: *mercury's in retrograde*
    & *turquoise is an emotion* & *ugh bring me baaack*
but i've read the farmer's almanac   i'm on the outs
    with change, eating a soul-destroying meal—
twinkies, register fruit—at a gas station, in a golden hour
    that is well-intentioned   & that's the time
to reflect, to think about what we desire most:
    is it a cool linen vernacular or to be this
old bitter girl who lives in the blueish
    grasp between winter   & more winter?

Brief List of Things That Will Kill Me

ii. this vessel

The see-through kind: anatomy, a shell, a ship
steering on a long-winded line between pale blue

and a lemon peel I must've sucked dry;

but my internal weather is a Northeast winter
stuck on a birdshit-covered rock on the edge

of the world as rain pounds down on the lighthouse,

waves crash, seagulls scream and orbit about me
like Saturn's rings because it is I, the salty old broad,

who tends the light, shovels in the coal:

keeper of sea shanties, tall tales, merfolk,
and you couldn't shut me up if you tried; as if

my skull wasn't encrusted with barnacles, tentacles,

mouth wasn't stuffed with a corncob pipe—aye,
if boredom is the devil's plaything, make me a swing—

I'm already in tilt and sway between kerosene martini

and rant, aria and spill the beans, already in rivalry
with my understudy—bunny-slippered ego that follows

me with a shovel—with Melville, that sonovabitch,

with the moon's sparkle on the pitch-black sea while
I swab, swab, swab the spiral staircase leading to light,

and I don't mean to upset the natural order or anything

but when might I get to play Prometheus? give myself
to the birds? Sometimes, a girl needs a little salvation

from feeling like Charybdis, from glimpsing luminescent

calm overhead—it's been 1500 weeks and I'm trying
to wield my body like a captain does the storm

and when I say *foghorn*, I mean *cleave me*
                              from these bones.

Ghosthood

& it feels like lying on a bed
      like a heap of winter coats during a dinner party to be sought-after when needed

as if I'm surrounded by a floor full of white sheets
          all sulk & piss-off
               & I have nothing to wear

& when I finally make an appearance, there is no Freddie Prinze Jr. waiting
             at the foot of the staircase

through my eyeholes, I see the rounds of mint juleps, cocktail weenies
        & how my mood lingers over guests like dead metaphor
            like lake mist

& there must be some kind of cosmic explanation
        for ephemeral flesh

so far, there is no fade-to-black, no pottery sculpting, no Long Island medium in the afterlife
      just me trying to morse code a candlestick's drip
        aches through a door's creak

& I'm sopping wet in someone else's grief, spineless, asking the grandfather clock to gong
        keep going, going

wringing out my moth-bitten soul as the saddest exhibit
      of flambéing Baked Alaska takes place

& it is exhausting to be in a time loop of morning light slow-dancing on the kitchen hutch
      being tied to these lace curtains
      in Schenectady & you,

my love—did you like the paranormal doilies I've left? the dust I kissed onto the asters?
    I would drag a UFO through a keyhole

to say *I am safe*, but when I am walking
    I never reach the walls

Chop Suey

Edward Hopper, 1929

Even Hopper couldn't stop her.
I hate how her chopsticks puncture
water chestnut—a misophonic crystal
rises like jagged bottom teeth. I hate
her dumb fork scratching white plate.
It's her cosmic lust I distrust.
Face-to-face, rook-to-rook—a chasm,

a table between us—puff puff pass—
I laugh at my faux-fur doppelgänger
as she sizes me up, thinks she can replace
a queen. I'm no fool. I know those ringlet
thoughts that drip from dark places: hideous
stalactites, amethyst & slug. A thug who
pulls the rug out from nurture & harm.

Dream Vision of Sylvia Plath

love had me reeling since the lake, the headlong plunge into barren landscape, where ranks of rolling hills are guarded by black cypress that slant toward bishops. staggering about no man's land as my rival puzzles over her next move. she bites a fat purple fig then drops it to snowmelt. *I stalk like a rook* with dark plumes, perfumed and molting each style like a sable fur coat. my empress preens in expensive taste. I clip on her unwashed braid and feel like a Clydesdale galloping into my thirties; the annihilating brute whiff of what it means to "have it all—" baby books and dissertations, boss bitch and stinking bibs. *consolation?* she asks, offering her remedies, her nightshades. I peel my cuticles like eggshells, like archaic wallpaper. who mothered who? dressed me in footie pajamas and laid me down upon the forest floor? was this Plath's gambit? the unseen latticework of hyphae: *overnight, very whitely, discreetly, very quietly our toes, our noses take hold on the loam, acquire the air.* we lodge ourselves as truffles, as dreams, adjourned. as wet season spawn with soft fists breaking into Egyptian cotton, the dormant generation becomes sinewy from crumbs, sweeps tidy tercets into the dustbin, heaves through dried leaves, unexcused, not needing light, though a little is nice. we rise like gilled pillars—matsutake, hen-of-the-woods—slightly restored, but colossal. as grandmasters of the undergrowth, we inherit stately oak rooms; patient for the poem to swell in the night, up, up toward full-throated spring

Donut Shop Pantoum

It's a sad day, the counter girl says, *we're all out.*
But even on National Donut Day it don't matter to me; sticky
sweet goes down like a jagged pill without water. The orange
of this place—Golden Gate Bridge, persimmon—a pigment

of anguish. A national holiday? I'm here only to rhyme *dough*
with *Rimbaud*, to be alone with Mrs. Butterworth's & styrofoam.
The cash-only sign's color is that of Carrot Top, Mario Batali's crocs.
I never read *The Odyssey,* but I think I get the gist

as I swim alone in a sea of styrofoam & high-fructose corn syrup.
In this Indiana trash town, I watch coffee drip from delicate
instruments, thinking of Homer Simpson with a fluorescent lyre
& deep-fried, glazed hole of *d'oh!* yelling *O small,*

tortured town, you are the apricot-stuff of poetry—machinery-gunk
color like circus peanuts, bad spray tans, prescription bottles.
Empty trays of glazed O's behind her, she goes for the jugular:
It's a sad day, the counter girl says to a regular, *we're all out.*

Birds!

There won't be a cage in this poem. Suppose hummingbirds
Glitched from Yucatán over the border in a silk-thread
Existence. Birds of prey collided with the Chrysler Building.
Suppose it is end times & bad omens washed amuck in marsh,
Appalachia, the East Coast. Suppose pelicans & gulls dropped
Like stones, bloodied eyes & beaks—the Audubon Society
Turned to taxidermy. Suppose birds forgot magnetic pull,
Forgot how to fly in V's, in Charlie Parker rhythms. Suppose outside
Was bare as a white room & birdsong was bottled for pleasure.
Then, I'd be Marion Crane—back from the dead, feathered mimicry.
Been locked up in a dark closet like a Furby—going back & forth
To the drive-thru for a Crunchwrap Supreme, wondering where
My magpie boo-thing has gone? Fattened up on blackberry, but
Hungry for the fall of wave & cloud on a little house by the sea.

Lolita Licking Wounds

after Kate Clark's Tale

As once sheepish sprites who skipped school inside empty
water towers—those dewlapped & bright-bellied things—
born pure as clotted cream to be signed away on the dotted line

as "Lo. Lee. Ta." chopped-up & served to the palette like tartare,
spat out into cloth napkins & later become novel. Queens-to-Be
with a cherry-stem aesthetic, touching the linguistic G-spot,

le petite mort. We have tongued our most precious lacerations
because Cher Horowitz ruled it so: "Anything you can do to draw
attention to your mouth is good." But if you stalk our schoolgirl slacks,

Dutch braid slithering between knob knees, you'll find we've snapped
the heart-shaped sunglasses & our long-sought-after loins were razor-
burned since the opening lines. Now, we turn three times before

settling, lying low in overgrown, unfostered grass with front legs
bent inward. Our moan grows & grows like ragweed. If we arrive
upon the eve of our thirtieth birthday, we will eat ice cream cake,

daydrink & backstroke through quarter-life crises (surely,
Humbert Humbert will wince at us like week-old lettuce).
If our moods feel like storm surge pounding a seawall,

we will bisect from girlness, girlmess. Unflinching, but mangy,
we pant into pastoral pelts, into not-self. Our art must be alchemical,
a salve. We taxidermy our bodies into arrow-torn hides: bighorn

curving in place of braids, but keeping medieval pouts. Our art
must be fanged, yellow-eyed & preying on Nabokov inside
the study's warmth with rabid desire for his head over the mantle.

No longer jilted creatures consoling ourselves, separated
from our hooves: the language lent here will outlast you
as the wayward *we* lean toward the chainlink & mist.

"Drawbridge + Moat" is dedicated to Marianne Moore's "Black Earth."

"Deadbeat Beach" is after Cate Marvin's poem "Dread Beach" with its catalog of trash on Staten Island, New York, beaches. It includes a quote from Adrienne Rich's "Diving into the Wreck."

"The Promenade, Brooklyn Heights" references films set in New York City such as *When Harry Met Sally* (Columbia Pictures, 1989); *Moonstruck* (Metro-Goldwyn-Mayer, 1987); and *Annie Hall* (Metro-Goldwyn-Mayer, 1977).

The Dream Vision series recites and playfully repurposes the writing of influential poets by using italicized language to point toward their direct quotations.

"Shitshow Barbie" is influenced by Natalie Diaz's "The Last Mojave Indian Barbie" and Denise Duhamel's *Kinky* (Orchises, 1997).

"Bees!" references the texts *Silent Spring* (Mariner Books Classics, 2022) by Rachel Carson and *Slow Violence and the Environmentalism of the Poor* (Harvard University Press, 2013) by Rob Nixon. The titles "Bees!," "Parks!," and "Birds!" are influenced by Upton Sinclair's *Oil!* and Danez Smith's series in *Homie* (Graywolf Press, 2020).

"Lust-Drunk" incorporates a line from *Seinfeld's* "The Mango" (Season 5, Episode 1; September 16, 1993).

The "Elegy for Anthony Bourdain" epigraph is a quote from Bourdain in the essay "Don't Eat Before Reading This." It includes a line from the television series *Parts Unknown* (CNN, 2013), when he visited South Africa.

"Brief List of Things That Will Kill Me: Being Favored" is inspired by Yorgos Lanthimos' *The Favourite* (Searchlight Pictures, 2018).

"Consider the Lobster Telephone" alludes to Salvador Dalí's Surrealist object *Lobster Telephone*, as well as David Foster Wallace's essay "Consider the Lobster" (*Gourmet Magazine*, 2004).

"Advice Column" mentions performance art titled *Mattress Performance (Carry That Weight)* by Emma Sulkowicz.

The "Viciousness in the Kitchen" title is lifted from Sylvia Plath's poem "Lesbos" and includes a quote from "Cut."

The "Take My Milk" title is from Shakespeare's Lady Macbeth in Act I, Scene V, when she declares, "Come to my woman's breasts, / And take my milk for gall." Poem includes a quote from Frank Bidart's "Ellen West."

"Swampland with Red Solo Cups" is dedicated to Alice Bolin's essay collection *Dead Girls: Essays on Surviving an American Obsession* (HarperCollins, 2018). It employs a quote from John Keats' "Ode to a Nightingale" and references many films and television shows such as *Kill Bill* (Miramax, 2003) and *Twin Peaks* (ABC, 1990).

"Brief List of Things That Will Kill Me: This Vessel" is inspired by Robert Eggers' film *The Lighthouse* (A24, 2019).

"Lolita Licking Wounds" references a line from *Clueless*, which featured Alicia Silverstone as Cher Horowitz in an iconic adaptation of Jane Austen's *Emma* (Paramount Pictures, 1995).

Acknowledgments

Grateful acknowledgments to the editors of the following publications where early versions of these poems have appeared:

American Literary Review – "Bees!"

American Poetry Journal – "On Being Turquoise"

Best New Poets 2021 – "Nomenclature"

Black Warrior Review – "Drawbridge + Moat"

The Boiler – "The Girl with the Appetite of an Ogre"

Cimarron Review – "*Chop Suey*" & "Down, Down from Fenneltown"

The Cincinnati Review – "Lolita's Exorcism"

Copper Nickel – "Consider the Lobster Telephone"; "Ferry Song, Half-Sung" & "Lolita's Dissection"

DIAGRAM – "Advice Column"

Diode Poetry Journal – "Birds!" & "Peonies in Utero"

Fairy Tale Review – "On Becoming Bertha"

Fugue – "Dream Vision of Elizabeth Bishop"

The Harvard Advocate – "Dream Vision of Sylvia Plath"

Hayden's Ferry Review – "Brief List of Things That Will Kill Me: Being Favored"

Hobart Pulp – "Dream Vision of Frank O'Hara"

Josephine Quarterly – "Ghosthood"

Laurel Review – "Swampland with Red Solo Cups"

Meridian – "Collective Invention"

Mississippi Review – "Viciousness in the Kitchen"

Muzzle – "Dyker Heights, 2017"

Painted Bride Quarterly – "Q Train"

Peach Mag – "Dream Vision Descending Into Dickinson"

The Pinch – "Bubbly + Cake," "Deadbeat Beach," "Gnaw at the Orchids" & "Lust-Drunk"

Plume – "Dream Vision of Theodore Roethke"

Poet Lore – "Elegy for Anthony Bourdain"

Protean Magazine – "Hieronymus Bosch's *The Garden of Earthly Delights*"

Puerto del Sol – "Juniper + Chest of Apples"

The Rumpus – "Girl in Bathtub, Flicking Dried Rose Petal"

Salt Hill – "Shitshow Barbie"

South Dakota Review – "Pomegranate Inn, Portland, Maine" & "The Promenade, Brooklyn Heights"

Southern Indiana Review – "Brief List of Things That Will Kill Me: This Vessel"

Storm Cellar – "Fever Dream Vision of Allen Ginsberg"

Sugar House Review – "Donut Shop Pantoum"

Third Coast – "The Curious Sadness of Sugar Cone"

VIDA Review – "Parks!"

Yalobusha Review – "Portrait of a Queen with Dirty Martini, Covered in Cat Hair"

Thank you to Ron Mitchell, Rosalie Moffett, and Amie Whittemore for reading proofs.

Thank you to judge Michael Waters for selecting this book.

Thank you to all of my poetry buds at Florida State University—Brett Hanley, KT, Isabella Tommasone, Brett Cortelletti, Will Anderson, Lauren Howton, Emilio Carrero, Zuleyha Ozturk, and Max Lasky—who were always down to talk shop under the live oaks.

Thank you to my teachers for all your guidance, babka & preserves: Cate Marvin, Micheal Schuyler, Tyehimba Jess, Alessandra Lynch, Chris Forhan, Hilene Flanzbaum, David Shumate, Barbara Hamby, Virgil Suarez, David Kirby, and Jimmy Kimbrell.

Thank you thank you thank you to my very Italian family—Michael, Michele, Nicole—for your endless love and support, for never doubting me.

Lastly, thank you to Anthony for sitting next to me in the workshop circle in Staten Island, Indianapolis, Tallahassee, and wherever next, for following me through all the realms.

Natalie Louise Tombasco is a poet, editor, and teacher from Staten Island, NY. Tombasco holds an MFA from Butler University and a PhD in creative writing from Florida State University. She is a visiting assistant professor at the University of Tampa. Recent work can be found in *Best New Poets*, *Verse Daily*, *Gulf Coast*, *Black Warrior Review*, *Diode Poetry Journal*, *Copper Nickel*, and *The Cincinnati Review*, among others. Find out more at *natalielouisetombasco.com*.

The Michael Waters Poetry Prize was established in 2013 to honor Michael's contributions to *Southern Indiana Review* and American arts and letters.

Previous MWPP Winners

2022—Chelsea Woodard

2021—Bethany Schultz Hurst

2020—Erin Rodoni

2019—Julia Koets

2018—Chelsea Wagenaar

2017—Marty McConnell

2016—Ruth Awad

2015—Annie Kim

2014—Dennis Hinrichsen & Hannah Faith Notess

2013—Doug Ramspeck

Southern
Indiana
Review
Press